# Pri ꜱ sh: Audit and Test

# Achieving QTS

## Primary English: Audit and Test
### Assessing your knowledge and understanding

## Fourth Edition

## Sue Reid, Angela Sawyer and Mary Bennett-Hartley

⑤SAGE | LearningMatters

Los Angeles | London | New Delhi
Singapore | Washington DC

Learning Matters
An imprint of SAGE Publications Ltd
1 Oliver's Yard
55 City Road
London EC1Y 1SP

SAGE Publications Inc.
2455 Teller Road
Thousand Oaks, California 91320

SAGE Publications India Pvt Ltd
B 1/I 1 Mohan Cooperative Industrial Area
Mathura Road
New Delhi 110 044

SAGE Publications Asia-Pacific Pte Ltd
3 Church Street
#10-04 Samsung Hub
Singapore 049483

Editor: Amy Thornton
Production controller: Chris Marke
Project management: Deer Park Productions, Tavistock, Devon
Marketing manager: Catherine Slinn
Cover design: Wendy Scott
Typeset by: C&M Digitals (P) Ltd, Chennai, India
Printed by: Henry Ling Limited at The Dorset Press, Dorchester, DT1 1HD

© 2014 Doreen Challen, Sue Reid, Angela Sawyer, Mary Bennett-Hartley

First published in 2001 by Learning Matters Ltd

Reprinted in 2002. Second edition published in 2003. Reprinted in 2003, 2004, 2005, 2006.

Third edition published in 2007. Reprinted in 2007, 2008, 2009, 2010, 2011. Fourth edition published in 2014.

**Library of Congress Control Number: 2013954554**

**British Library Cataloguing in Publication Data**

A catalogue record for this book is available from the British Library

ISBN 978-1-4462-8275-5 (pbk)
ISBN 978-1-4462-8274-8

# Contents

# About the authors

**Sue Reid** is currently working part time at Newman University, Birmingham, as a senior lecturer in primary English on the PGCE and undergraduate programmes for initial teacher education. She also teaches on the third-year English specialism module for ITE students. Sue studied at Birmingham City University and worked in Birmingham schools for 20 years where she taught in every year group from Reception to Year 6. She took on management roles for a variety of subjects and eventually became subject leader for English in a large primary school on the outskirts of the city. During this time she gained a Master's degree in English, awarded by Birmingham University. Sue also worked as a lead teacher which led to her being appointed as a literacy consultant for the National Strategies in Worcestershire. This included supporting schools and leading training sessions in all aspects of English. Sue's areas of interest include the teaching of phonics and early reading, visual literacy and how to improve teachers' and students' classroom practice.

**Angela Sawyer** is currently working as a senior lecturer in primary English on both the PGCE and undergraduate programmes for initial teacher education and contributes to the Foundation Degree for Teaching and Learning at Newman University, Birmingham. After studying at Wolverhampton University, she spent many years teaching in a large inner-city primary school in Birmingham taking on extra management roles alongside a diverse range of curricular responsibilities. In 2009, after participating in a research project relating to visual literacy using Bollywood films, she developed an interest in the use of visual literacy to support learning amongst EAL learners. In 2012 she was appointed as a senior lecturer at Newman University and is currently completing her Masters dissertation. Her areas of interest include research into the use of ICT to support literacy, in particular the effectiveness of i-pads and developing the use of poetry in the classroom.

**Mary Bennett-Hartley** is currently working as a senior lecturer in primary education at Birmingham City University. Prior to this she taught primary English on both PGCE and undergraduate initial teacher education programmes at Newman University, Birmingham. Mary completed her undergraduate studies in English literature and linguistics at Bangor University; her PGCE (specialising in English) is from the University of Cambridge. She has taught across the age range in middle and primary schools in Worcestershire and Birmingham, undertaking additional curriculum and pastoral responsibilities. In 2006, Mary completed a Master's degree in English at the University of Birmingham, where her dissertation research explored attitudes to reading amongst Year 7 pupils. Mary's interests lie in regional accents and how these impact on the teaching of reading in primary schools and the use of children's literature in the classroom.

# Introduction

## About this book

This book has been written to support the subject knowledge learning of all primary trainee teachers on all courses of Initial Teacher Training (ITT) in England and other parts of the UK where a secure subject knowledge and understanding of English is required for the award of Qualified Teacher Status (QTS). In order to plan and teach effective English lessons, and to assess pupils' learning, it is vital that you yourself have a secure subject knowledge and understanding of how the English language works, and feel confident in this. The audit and test materials presented here, in seven sections, will help you to identify your own strengths and weaknesses in English. As you revise, you can revisit these to help you monitor and evaluate your own progress towards QTS:

**Part 1** Reflection on English: your experiences so far

**Part 2** Reflection on English: your perceptions

**Part 3** Perceived competence and confidence in English

**Part 4** English test

**Part 5** Answers to test questions

**Part 6** From subject knowledge to pedagogy

**Part 7** Targets for further development

**Part 8** Suggestions for revision and further reading

It is quite likely that your ITT provider will require you to further audit and test your subject knowledge and understanding of English as you start your course. You may wish to retain the results from this audit and test for your own records, using them for revision purposes. Your ITT provider may also wish to use them for their own records too.

You may feel confident that, as a sophisticated user of English, possibly already having completed a degree, you already meet or exceed the subject knowledge expectations for a primary teacher. If so, you should find the test easy, and can go on with added confidence to develop your teaching skills. On the other hand, you may feel rather daunted, perhaps because it's been some time since you thought about how the English language works, or because you're aware that there are many aspects required nowadays which you didn't learn at school yourself. If so, there's no need to worry. After you've carried out this audit and test, you'll be able to pinpoint those areas which you will need to study further if you are to feel confident in the classroom, and then you can start to address your particular needs.

If you wish to revise, or feel the need for an English study aid, there are several excellent books written specifically for this purpose for primary trainees. *Primary English: Knowledge and Understanding* (6th edn) from the Learning Matters QTS Series is particularly recommended. (See also the suggested reading in Part 8.)

# The Teachers' Standards for Qualified Teacher Status (2012)

New Teachers' Standards were introduced from 1 September 2012. The Standards set a clear baseline of expectations for the professional practice and conduct of teachers, from the point of qualification. They replace the standards for Qualified Teacher Status (QTS) and Core, and the GTCE's Code of Conduct and Practice for Registered Teachers in England.

The Teachers' Standards are used to assess all trainees working towards QTS, and all those completing their statutory induction period. They are also used to assess the performance of all teachers subject to the Education (School Teachers' Appraisal) (England) Regulations 2012. Primary trainees are required to meet all the eight standards in order to be awarded QTS. The Standards include, as aspects of professional knowledge and understanding, the requirements for trainee teachers to know and understand not only the revised National Curriculum for English, but also to consider the wider implications of teaching English in the 21st century.

In terms of the professional skills set out in the Standards, it is vital that your subject knowledge is sufficiently secure for you to feel confident in teaching and assessing children's learning. Strong subject knowledge will enable you to understand the concepts you teach, so that you can explain them appropriately and offer examples to clarify, helping your pupils to investigate and explore their own understanding. Strong subject knowledge will enable you to identify specifically what your pupils can already achieve and ensure that you plan effectively in order to demonstrate focused teaching and progression for each individual. It will also help you to devise questions and provide feedback to move the learning on.

The audit and test materials in this book include many aspects of the specific English subject knowledge which you will need to know and understand in order to plan, teach and assess across Key Stages 1 and 2. The Standards also require you to take responsibility for addressing your own personal and professional development through identifying and meeting your own targets. This book, by helping you to identify particular areas of subject knowledge for further study, has been designed to help you do this more effectively for English.

The audit and test materials cover:

- **the nature and role of standard English;**
- **the spoken and written language systems of English at word, sentence and text levels;**
- **how to evaluate texts and language critically;**
- **technical terms necessary to discuss English.**

# English: the National Curriculum for England

The original National Curriculum was introduced to all maintained schools throughout England and Wales for the first time in 1989. This was revised in 1999 and again in 2013 and at the time of writing, this revised version is in the course of being implemented in schools. From September 2014 maintained schools have a statutory duty to teach the new curriculum (see references). English in the 2014 National Curriculum is organised year by year for Years 1 and 2 and in two-year phases for Lower KS2

# Finished Creature

## Resources
- Children's creature images from the previous activity
- Image manipulation software

### Starting Points

Look at the printouts of the creatures on the different backgrounds. Discuss how adding details, such as shadows and other effects might make the image look more dramatic. Demonstrate how different tools in the **image manipulation software**, such as pencil and paintbrush, can be used to add detail, and how filter effects can change the look of the image.

### Approach

1. Ask the children to modify their pictures by applying a filter effect to selected parts of the image.

2. Experiment with shadow, lighting and proportion effects to help 'blend' the image into the photograph.

3. Add some colour to selected parts of the image using the paint tool.

4. Experiment with distortion effects to give drama to the image.

5. Save and print the final image.

# Object Walk

### Resources
- White paper
- Charcoal
- Pencils
- Coloured pencils
- Pastels
- Sketchbooks
- Digital camera
- Computer connected to the Internet

*Reclining Figure*, edition of six by Henry Moore (1898–1986), 1969–70 (bronze) by Henry Spencer Moore (1898–1986) Belverdere, Florence, Italy/Bridgeman Art Library

## Starting Points

Talk about the ways in which artists use natural forms as a starting point for sculpture. Use the Internet to find out about Henry Moore, Andy Goldsworthy and Richard Long (website suggestion page 72), all of whom use natural forms as a starting point for developing sculptural ideas. Go for a walk around the local environment and collect and make drawings of objects such as fragments of wood, stones, and so on. Take photographs of the local environment where the objects were found using a **digital camera**.

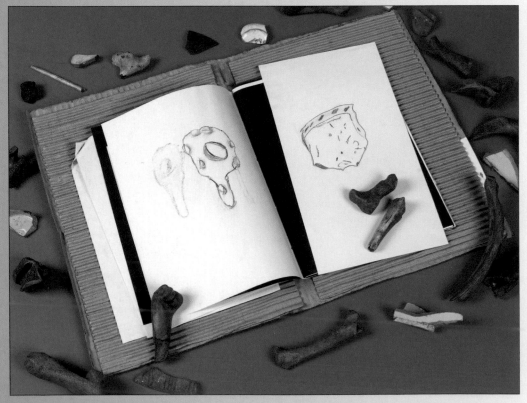

## Approach

1. Look closely at the objects on the walk. Discuss the different shapes and forms. Ask the children to imagine what the object would look like if it was made on a large scale and placed in the environment as a sculpture. Use the sculptures of Henry Moore and Andy Goldsworthy as a reference.

2. Draw a large-scale picture of one of the objects. Experiment with different viewpoints, using a mixture of charcoal, pencil and pastels.

# Building the Sculptures

## Resources

- Computer connected to the Internet
- Children's charcoal drawings from the previous activity
- Cardboard, corrugated card or assortment of wood off-cuts
- Newspaper, masking tape and papier-mâché
- Glue, tape or wire
- String
- Coloured tissue paper
- Beads
- Foil
- Paints

## Starting Points

Demonstrate a range of techniques for constructing large shapes out of scrap material. Talk about how sculptural structures can be formed using different medias such as wire, card or wood. Look again at the images of sculptures found on the Internet. Discuss the different materials used. What materials would work best for the children's own sculptures?

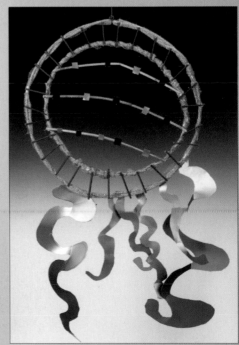

## Approach

1. Ask the children to look at their charcoal drawings of objects from the previous activity. Choose one drawing to be made into a 3-D sculpture.

2. Decide which materials will be needed to make the sculpture and gather them together.

3. Use cardboard or wood to create a basic structure for tall sculptures, or crumpled newspaper wrapped with tape and covered with papier-mâché for more organic forms. Use tape, glue or wire to join shapes together.

4. Use string, coloured tissue, beads, foil and paints to decorate the forms.

# Virtual Sculptures

## Resources
- Digital camera
- Image manipulation software
- Children's completed 3-D sculptures from the previous activity

## Starting Points

Talk about how **image manipulation software** can be used to enhance or change the features of a 3-D sculpture. Demonstrate how to use the **digital camera** to take a photograph of a child's sculpture. Load this image onto the computer and show how the colour and form of the sculpture can be changed using the software tools.

## Approach

1. Using a digital camera, take photographs of the sculpture against a neutral background (to make it easier to cut out).

2. Experiment with **colour filters**.

3. Explore other ways of manipulating the image, such as changing its size.

4. Save and print each example and display showing the sequence of the manipulated image.

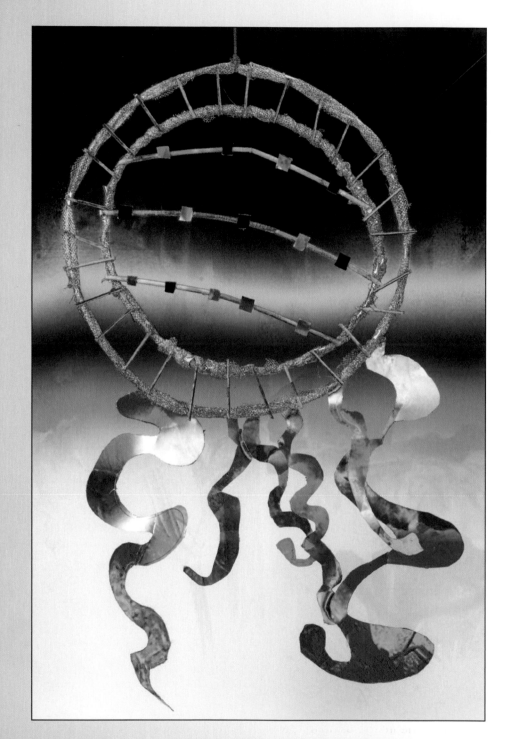

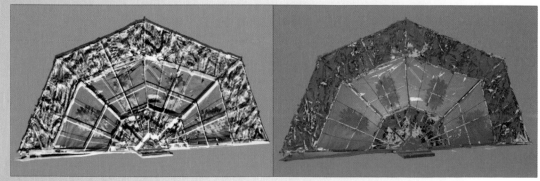

# Sculptures in the Environment

## Resources
- Digital photographs of the local environment from the activity on page 16
- Digital photographs of manipulated sculptures from the previous activity
- Image manipulation software

## Starting Points

Show the children the digital images of the local environment. Explain that by using **image manipulation software**, the children's sculptures can be placed into an environment. Refer again to the work of Henry Moore, Richard Long and Andy Goldsworthy. Demonstrate how to cut out a digital sculpture image and place it onto a digital photograph. Talk about how the **layer feature** allows the sculpture to be moved around and scaled up or down. Discuss how a layer can be modified or duplicated without affecting the background.

## Approach

1. Load a sculpture image and **flatten** the image to combine all of the layers.

2. Edit the background of the image so that the sculpture can be seen against a white screen.

3. Save the image using a new name.

4. Load a digital photograph of the local environment.

5. Copy and paste the sculpture image onto the image of the local environment. Scale the image of the sculpture up or down for dramatic effect.

6. Save this final image and print.

# Cave Paintings

*Cave Painting © Corel*

## Starting Points

The Internet is a large library at your fingertips. Explain to the children that many websites provide information about artists, designers from different periods in history. Demonstrate how to find information using a **search engine** and explain that this acts like a contents section in a book. Find pictures of cave paintings on the Internet (website suggestions on page 72).

## Approach

1. Look at the pictures of cave paintings. Talk about the images. What symbols can the children find? What do the symbols mean?

2. Use the pictures as a starting point for the creation of cave drawings. Draw symbols onto white art paper in black pen.

3. Display the drawings with the pictures of cave paintings. Add any written information that the children have found during their search on the Internet.

# Using Symbols

## Resources
- Computer connected to the Internet
- Pictures of cave paintings
- Paint software

## Starting Points

Discuss the difference between cave paintings and contemporary signs and symbols used in everyday life, such as traffic signs and **emoticons**. Explain how computer-generated **clip art** uses simplified outlines to convey meaning. Show some clip art symbols (website suggestions on page 72) to demonstrate how this is done. Explain that it is possible to create a collection of favourite clip art from the Internet.

## Approach

1. Find and explore a clip art site on the Internet (website suggestions on page 72).

2. After finding appropriate signs or symbols, ask the children to save them by pressing the right-hand mouse button on top of the clip art picture and then save it onto the hard disk.

3. Draw freehand cave symbols on the computer using the **mouse** and **art and design software**. Print out the symbols.

4. Compare and contrast the differences between the symbols used in cave paintings, those found on the clip art website and the freehand drawings.

# 3-D Cave Paintings

## Resources
- Pictures of cave paintings
- Sketchbooks
- Art paper (large size)
- Pencils
- Oil pastels in four earthy shades
- Paints
- Charcoal

## Starting Points

Look again at the pictures of cave paintings. Split the class into groups and give each group a name of an imaginary tribe, for example bears, eagles or bulls. Explain that each group should invent some symbols that best represent their tribe. Ask the children to record their ideas in a sketchbook.

## Approach

1. Ask the groups to crumple the art paper carefully into a ball.

2. Gently unwrap the paper, flatten it and tape the corners on to a table (this will give the effect of an uneven rock surface).

3. Ask each group to choose a selection of symbols from the sketchbooks. Each group member should then carefully draw a symbol on to the paper in charcoal.

4. Use the oil pastels (earthy shades) and paints to complete the composition.

# Making 3-D Boulders

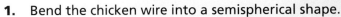

## Starting Points

Discuss where in the world cave paintings appear. Talk about creating a rock display in the classroom. What materials could be used to create a 3-D effect?

## Approach

1. Bend the chicken wire into a semispherical shape.

2. Using thin strips of newspaper (3cms by 30cms – prepared in advance), overlay the strips onto the outside of the chicken wire framework with thin PVA glue. Alternatively, you can use strips of Modroc (fabric coated with plaster of Paris). When water is applied to Modroc strips, it will mould onto the wire frame surface.

3. Allow the boulders to dry for at least two days.

4. Paint the surface with an appropriate stone colour using water-based paint and allow to dry.

5. Using the children's sketchbooks as a reference, carefully draw or paint symbols onto the 3-D surface.

6. Compare and contrast the difference between working in two and three dimensions.

# Drawing Machine Parts

## Resources

- Computer connected to the Internet
- A collection of reclaimed machine parts
- Photocopier
- Scissors
- Glue
- White paper
- Charcoal
- Erasers
- Pencils
- White paint
- Colour printer

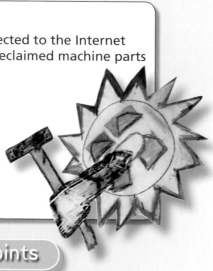

## Starting Points

Many artists have used recycled materials in their work. Collect and show a range of different reclaimed materials, for example machine parts, scrap material and old computer circuit boards. Find information on the Internet about Clayton Bailey and Vladimir Yankilevski, two artists who create robotic structures from reclaimed materials (website suggestion on page 72). Look at images of their work and discuss how the machine parts are used.

*Torso* by Vladimir Yankilevski (b. 1938), 1965 (oil, metal and wood).
Private collection/Bridgeman Art Library © ADAGP, Paris and DACS, London 2003

## Approach

1. Ask the children to look carefully at the machine parts. Discuss the different qualities of the shapes.

2. Place each machine part on the photocopier and make several copies.

3. Ask the children to select photocopies, cut them out and stick them onto a white sheet of paper.

4. Then prompt the children to draw bold outlines around the images using charcoal.

5. Use an eraser to rub out parts of the charcoal drawing to add different tones to the image, and use dark pencils and white paint to add detail and contrast.

6. Display the drawings as a backdrop to the collection of machine parts and pictures by relevant artists found during the Internet search.

# Designing a Robot

## Resources
- Computer connected to the Internet
- White paper
- Pencils
- Machine line drawings from the previous activity
- Black felt-tip pens
- Photocopier
- Pastels
- Collage materials (tin foil, buttons, beads, wire)
- Glue

## Starting Points

Look again at pictures by Clayton Bailey on the Internet (website suggestion on page 72). Talk about the ways in which he has used different shapes and materials to construct the robots. Ask the class to think about the overall shape and the details that make up the head, body and limbs.

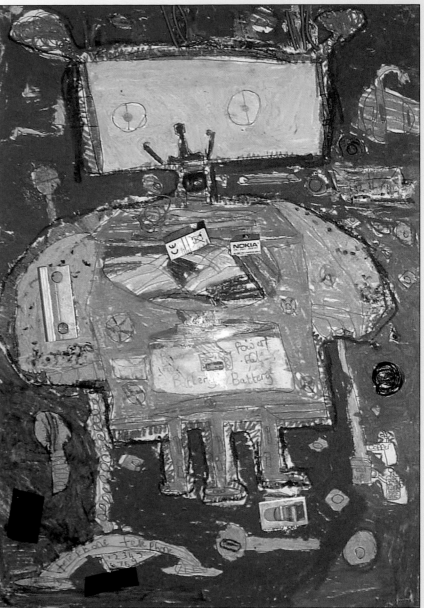

## Approach

1. Ask the children to make a pencil sketch of a fantastic robot.

2. Add details using the machine drawings for ideas. Draw using lines only.

3. When the robot is complete, go around the outline using a black felt-tip pen.

4. Make photocopies of the robot drawings.

5. Using a photocopy of the drawing, add colour, pattern and detail to the robot using pastels.

6. Collage 'real' machine parts on to the robot using wire, buttons, beads and tin foil.

# Creating a Digital Robot

## Resources
- Children's photocopies of robot drawings
- Collection of reclaimed machine parts
- Digital camera
- Scanner
- Image manipulation software

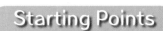

## Starting Points

Look again at the collection of reclaimed machine parts. Discuss with the children how the computer can be used to develop their robot designs to include images of these parts. Involve the children in photographing each machine part with the **digital camera** and demonstrate how to load these images on to the computer.

## Approach

1. Demonstrate how to **scan** a child's outline drawing of a robot into the computer.

2. Open the file containing the digital machine images. **Cut and paste** sections of the machine part images into the robot drawing.

3. Continue to cut and paste machine parts until the robot is complete. Save and print the image at different stages to show the development of the idea.

4. Choose a background colour and add this to the final design. Save and print.

# Developing a 3-D Robot

## Resources

- Pictures by Clayton Bailey used in the previous activities
- Children's robot drawings from the activity on page 25
- Chicken wire
- Cardboard
- Boxes
- Glue
- Scrap materials (paper, wire, balsa wood, foil, bottle tops, art straws, buttons)
- Circuit boards
- Metallic paint
- Foil

## Starting Points

Look again at the work of Clayton Bailey, who uses reclaimed materials in his art, and discuss with the children how they might build a robot. Talk about scale and how the robot might look from different viewpoints. Ask the children to look at their original robot drawings and examine the scrap materials. Discuss the different ways in which the materials could be used.

## Approach

1. Work in groups of four or five to develop a drawing for a 3-D robot. Encourage the children to refer to ideas from their previous drawings.

2. Demonstrate how a structure for the robot can be made using chicken wire and cardboard. Show the children how to join the wire and cardboard to create a robot shape.

3. Use a range of scrap materials to make the robot look interesting. Add panels which have been made separately using card and collage materials such as wire, art straws and balsa wood.

4. Consider the robot's features – eyes, nose, and mouth – and use suitable scrap materials to complete these details.

5. Remind the children to look at the robot from all sides and to add details so that it is interesting from all viewpoints.

# Mixed Media Prints

## Resources

- Computer connected to the Internet
- Roll of acetate
- Tape
- Water-based printing ink and rollers
- Paper
- Coloured tissue paper

*Birds Disturbing the Sleep of a Town* by Bryan Wynter (1915–1975), 1948 (monotype and gouache on paper)
35.5 x 50.7cm, Collection Newlyn Art Gallery, Cornwall UK © Estate of Bryan Wynter 2003. All Rights Reserved, DACS

## Starting Points

Talk to the children about mixed media art, where an artist uses more than one type of material in a work. Find images by mixed media artists on the Internet (website suggestions on page 72).

One example is Bryan Wynter, who combines printmaking and painting to create his landscapes. In the painting above, Wynter uses a monoprint background onto which he draws and paints landscape details such as trees, houses and birds.

## Approach

1. To make a mixed media monoprint, tape a length of acetate to a table surface.

2. Squeeze a 12cm line of coloured printing ink onto the acetate. Using an ink roller, spread the ink to create a rectangular shape.

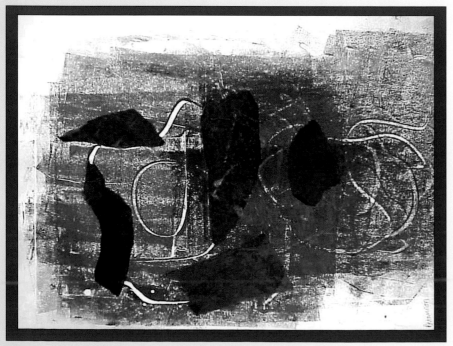

3. Use the edge of the roller to inscribe textural marks in the ink. Place a sheet of paper over the ink and apply pressure using a clean, dry roller.

4. Carefully peel the paper away from the acetate. Roll different coloured ink on to the acetate and repeat the above process several times.

5. Tear pieces of tissue paper into shapes and position them carefully onto the wet print.

6. Gently apply pressure so that the tissue paper will stay in place.

7. Allow the acetate to dry and use it as part of a display to show the printing process.

# Colour Filter Prints

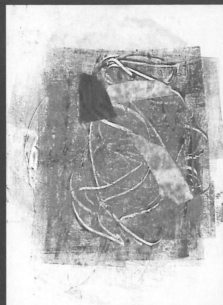  

## Resources
- Image manipulation software
- Mixed media prints
  from the previous activity
- Digital camera

Starting Points

Printmakers explore colour through making more than one print, using different papers and coloured inks. Talk about how the computer can change the colours of original prints and paintings with **image manipulation software**. Demonstrate the **colour filter** tools and discuss the various effects that can be achieved digitally.

## Approach

1. Ask the children to record their mixed media print using the **digital camera**. Load these images onto the computer.

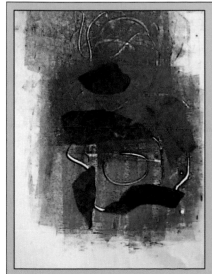 

2. Open a digital image and experiment with the colour filters to create different effects.

3. Create at least three different coloured digital prints, saving and printing each image.

4. Compare the computer printouts with the original mixed media monoprints and discuss the differences.

5. Display the original mixed media prints alongside the printouts to show the development of the work.

# Creating an Acetate Bird

## Resources

- Computer connected to the Internet
- Pencils
- Art paper
- Single acetate sheets suitable for printer
- Children's mixed media prints from the activity on page 28
- Paint software
- Overhead projector

## Starting Points

Artists often include details such as people and animals in a landscape. For an example, look at the mixed media work of Bryan Wynter (website suggestion on page 72). This extra detail adds a sense of life, movement and presence to artists' work. Look out of the window and discuss any landscape details that can be seen, such as people, wildlife, buildings and trees.

## Approach

1. Ask the children to produce several pencil drawings of birds in different positions in their sketchbooks.

2. Using the **mouse**, draw one bird in black line only. Ensure that the image fills the screen. Use the zoom tool to draw details.

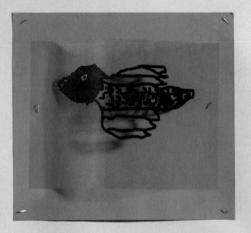
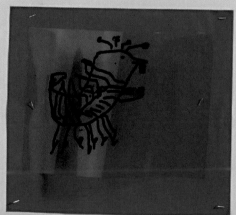

3. Save the bird and print out the image onto an acetate sheet. Alternatively, you can photocopy a paper printout of the bird onto acetate.

4. Place the digital acetate on to the original mixed media print. Show how the acetate can be moved about on the print. Decide on the best position for the acetate.

5. Alternatively, use an overhead projector to project the acetate printout onto a mixed media print on the wall. Several acetates can be projected at once so that the whole class can be involved in decisions about composition.

# Multimedia Landscape

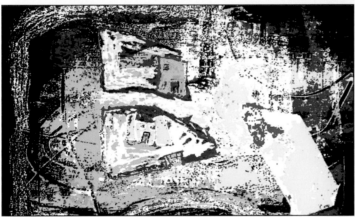

## Resources
- Oil pastels and crayons
- Children's mixed media prints from the activity on page 28
- Children's acetate birds from the previous activity
- Transparent tape
- Digital camera
- Image manipulation software

## Starting Points

Make a list of the features of the landscape around school such as trees, buildings and other landmarks.

## Approach

1. Use crayons and oil pastels to add detail to the mixed media print, turning it into a landscape.

2. Decide on the best position for the digital acetate printout of the bird and use transparent tape to secure the acetate onto the mixed media landscape.

3. Record the final print using a **digital camera**.

4. Load the images onto the computer and save.

5. Open one of the digitally recorded prints. Experiment with the **colour filters** to create different-coloured digital prints.

6. Create at least three different coloured digital prints, saving the results each time and printing them out.

7. Compare the new manipulated landscape prints with the original print.

# Pop Banner

## Resources
- Computer connected to the Internet
- Large roll of drawing paper (approximately 180cms by 180cms)
- Masking tape
- Wax crayons
- Coloured pastels

## Starting Points

Artists have always regarded portraiture as one of their greatest challenges. Today it is possible to use digital photography as a tool to record portraits, which can be further manipulated through **art and design software**. Pop artists, such as Eduardo Paolozzi, Tom Phillips and Andy Warhol, are famous for their use of bright colours and text.

## Approach

1. Search for pictures by Eduardo Paolozzi, Tom Phillips and Andy Warhol on the Internet (website suggestion on page 72).

   Discuss the use of different colours, shapes and patterns within the work.

2. Roll out the paper and tape to the floor or wall.

3. Divide the paper into different sections. Four pupils work on each section.

4. Using the artists as a reference point, create pop art patterns using bright, contrasting colours.

5. This banner will be used as a background/backdrop for the digital pop portraits (page 35).

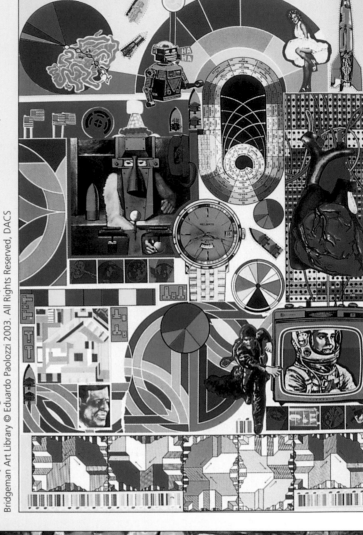

*B.A.S.H.* by Sir Eduardo Luigi Paolozzi (b. 1924), 1971 (print) The Potteries Museum and Art Gallery, Stoke on Trent, UK Bridgeman Art Library © Eduardo Paolozzi 2003. All Rights Reserved, DACS

# Creating a Pop Portrait

## Resources
- Thin card
- Scissors
- Digital camera
- Large white piece of paper
- Image manipulation software
- Coloured pencils and pastels

## Starting Points

Discuss the emotion you wish to show in your digital protrait. Create a small card picture frame to use as a viewfinder and explore different portrait compositions. Demonstrate how to record pictures using the **digital camera**.

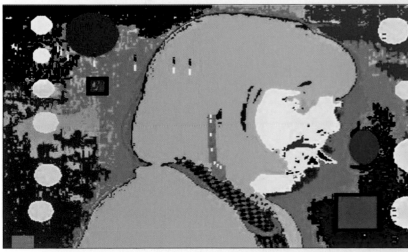

## Approach

1. Fix a large white piece of paper to the wall as a background for the portrait.

2. Ask the children to pose for a portrait. For example: happy, sad or thoughtful.

3. Record several versions of the portrait using the digital camera – front view, three-quarters view and profile. Load the images onto the computer.

4. Open and print a portrait using the **greyscale setting** on the printer.

5. Use coloured pencils and pastels to apply colour and pattern to the greyscale printout, creating an individual pop portrait.

6. Open another saved portrait and apply colour effects using a range of **colour filters**.

7. Add freehand detail with the **mouse** and experiment by filling areas with blocks of colour.

8. Use the text tool to write words on the portrait to depict the mood. Save and print the final portrait.

# Mask Making

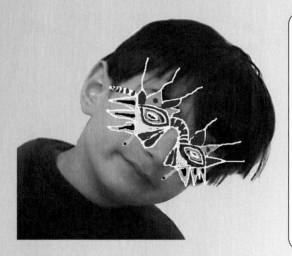

## Resources
- Computer connected to the Internet
- Thin card
- Ruler
- Pencils
- Scissors
- Coloured pencils or felt-tip pens
- String
- Tape
- Digital portraits from the previous activity (page 33)
- Image manipulation software

## Starting Points

Talk about creating a pop art mask. Look at some examples of masks found on the Internet (website suggestion page 72). Contemporary mask designers such as Judith Rauchfuss and Marie Coborn create masks using interesting forms and colours.

## Approach

1. Cut a mask shape out of card so that it will cover part of the face in an oval, rectangular or irregular shape.

2. Measure the distance between the eyes with a ruler, mark the position on the card with a pencil and then make two small holes with scissors.

3. Colour the mask with colourful pop art patterns.

4. To wear the mask, make two small holes on the edges and join with string.

5. Create a digital mask. Open a saved digital portrait. Use the magnifying tool to zoom into the eye area of the portrait, so that it fills the screen.

6. Set the paintbrush size to thin.

7. Design a virtual mask by drawing over the digital portrait using the **mouse**.

8. Save the different stages of the work. Zoom out and print.

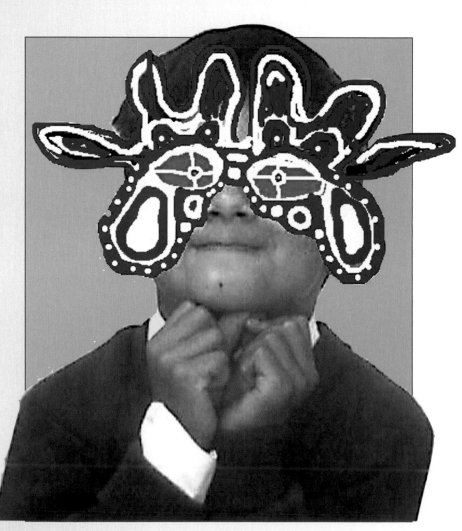

# Pop Art Scene

## Resources
- Pop art banner and masks from the previous activities
- Card viewfinder
- Digital camera
- Drawing pins

## Starting Points

Portrait work often provides an opportunity to discuss composition. Talk about creating a final pop art scene using the masks and banner. Where is the best place to stand when taking the photograph? At what angle should the mask-wearer stand and in what pose? Try out a variety of scenes, using the card viewfinder to assess composition. Take a picture with the **digital camera**.

## Approach

1. Position the pop art banner (page 32) on the wall in a spacious area of the classroom.

2. Ask children to stand in front of the pop art banner alone or in pairs.

3. Discuss presenting different emotions and actions in the poses.

4. Record several versions of the portrait composition.

5. As each picture is recorded, view the image in the camera and note the results; most digital cameras allow you to review the recorded pictures.

6. Load and save the pictures on the computer.

7. Print out the images.

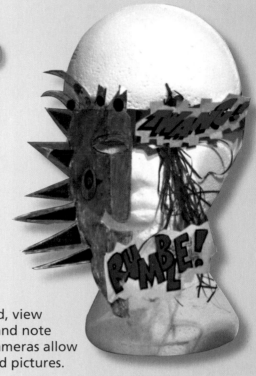

# Designing a Repeated Pattern

## Resources
- Examples of patterns by William Morris
- Products showing repeated patterns: wallpaper, wrapping paper
- Collection of leaves and flowers
- Image manipulation software
- Digital camera

*Daffodil* chintz designed by William Morris, c. 1875, Victoria & Albert Museum, London, UK/Bridgeman Art Library

## Starting Points

In the world of furnishing and fashion, computers play an increasingly important role. Explain to the children that designers often use the shapes and colours of natural forms, such as flowers in their work. Introduce the work of William Morris and talk about the repeated images in his designs. Show examples of repeated patterns on products such as wallpaper, wrapping paper, carpets and clothing. Explain that it is possible to create a repeated pattern using a **digital camera** and computer.

## Approach

1. Ask the children to photograph a selection of the leaves and flowers using the digital camera. Discuss issues relating to viewing and composing the picture.

2. Save the images onto the computer.

3. **Cut and paste** the images into the required repeated pattern and save.

4. Print out the designs and display alongside examples of commercially produced products that use repeated patterns.

# Exploring Pattern

## Resources
- Collection of leaves and flowers
- Computer connected to the Internet
- Image manipulation software
- Scanner

*Poppies* (oil on canvas) by Georgia O'Keefe (1887–1986), Private Collection Christie's Images/Bridgeman Art Library © ARS, NY and DACS, London 2003

## Starting Points

Artists and designers often use the natural world for their inspiration. Introduce the children to the work of Georgia O'Keefe (website suggestions page 72). Discuss how she uses images of the natural world.

## Approach

1. Put a single leaf into the scanner and copy the image onto the computer. The software should enable children to select the whole leaf or part of the leaf. The veins should become clearly visible.

2. **Scan** leaves of different shapes and colours into the computer, saving each image. Encourage the children to scan several flattened leaves at once to compose different images.

3. Decide which images to include in the design. Retrieve a saved image and **copy and paste** to create the pattern required. The software should allow the children to turn images on their vertical axis to produce a mirror effect.

4. Experiment by adding **colour filters**.

5. Print out the final design.

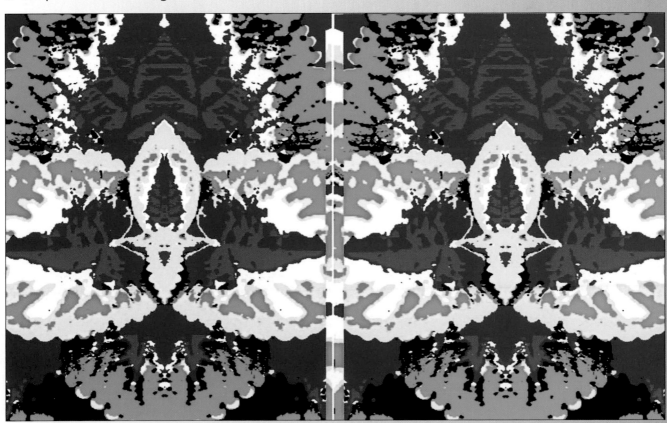

# T-Shirt Design

## Resources
- Textile inkjet paper
- Paint software
- Colour printer
- Plain T-shirts or fabric
- An iron

## Starting Points

If children do not have access to a scanner or **digital camera**, it is still possible to create a repeated pattern, such as a freehand flower drawing, using paint software. Discuss the functions of the art programme on your computer. The children would benefit from a demonstration, particularly of how to **cut and paste** images and how to use the paint fill tool.

## Approach

1. Draw a freehand flower motif with the **mouse**.

2. After saving the design, copy and paste the motif several times to create a repeated pattern.

3. Use the paint fill function to experiment with different colour variations.

4. Remind the children to save their final designs.

5. Print out the designs on to textile inkjet paper. The design can then be ironed on to T-shirts and displayed alongside printouts of the children's initial design motifs. Alternatively, iron the designs on to squares of fabric and sew the squares together to produce a wall hanging.

# Painting Patterns

## Resources

- Computer printouts of repeated patterns from the activity on page 36
- Watercolour paints
- Art paper

## Starting Points

Look at the pattern printouts and discuss recreating these images using paint and paper. How are digital methods different from traditional materials?

## Approach

1. Examine the computer printouts. Consider the most important colour in the image.

2. Create a light wash of paint in this colour over the central area of the paper. Allow to dry.

3. Draw in the outline using a thin paintbrush.

4. Paint in blocks of colour.

5. Compare the two techniques – traditional and digital. How is the end result different?

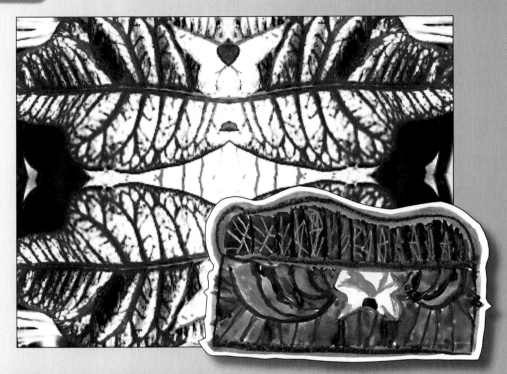

# Responding to Art

## Resources
- Computer connected to the Internet
- Examples of folk art
- Local newspaper
- Coloured art paper
- Charcoal and chalk

*Three Legged Dog Toasting Fork*, maker unknown, Late 18th or early 19th century.
Purchased by the Peter Moores Foundation for Display at Compton Verney, Warwickshire
© Compton Verney, photographed by Hugh Kelly

## Starting Points

Use the Internet to find out about folk art (website suggestion page 72). Folk art was made by relatively unskilled craftspeople who earned their living by selling their work. Many objects were produced to meet practical rather than artistic needs. Sometimes folk art paintings record an event. Look at some folk art, for example *Three Legged Dog Toasting Fork* (shown here). Encourage the children to be imaginative in their responses.

## Approach

1. Introduce the children to a local newspaper showing contemporary news and make a list of happy and sad news items.

2. Choose an event to record in charcoal. Encourage the children to think about the message that will be given through the artwork.

3. Alternatively, study a piece of folk art found on the Internet and ask the children to imagine that they are recording an event involving this object.

4. On a large piece of coloured art paper, draw a version of the event using charcoal and chalk.

# Recording a Scene

*Nine Angry Bulls*, artist unknown, c.1870, oil on canvas. Purchased by the Peter Moores Foundation for Display at Compton Verney, Warwickshire © Compton Verney, photographed by Hugh Kelly

## Resources
- Examples of folk art/local newspaper
- Digital camera
- Image manipulation software

## Starting Points

Look again at some folk art, for example *Nine Angry Bulls* (shown here). Discuss the feelings evoked in the pictures and the events that are recorded.

## Approach

1. Choose a folk painting or newspaper report and decide what feelings are evoked in the events or images.

2. Decide how this event could be portrayed then set up the scene or strike a pose and make faces to depict the different feelings and emotions.

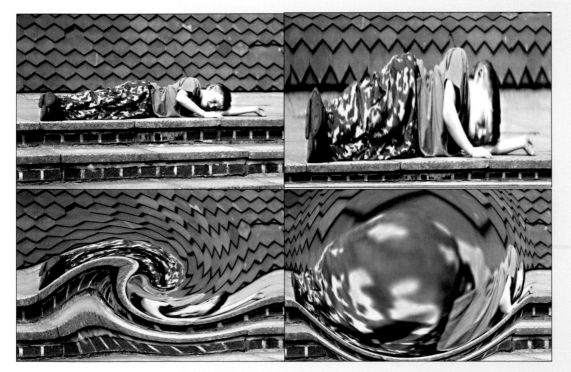

3. Use the **digital camera** to record several views of the scene.

4. Load the digital images on to the computer. Consider how image manipulation effects might enhance the emotions shown in the photograph. Experiment with the different effects such as stretching the image and changing its original shape.

5. Save and print out the results.

# Adding Colour Effects and Text

## Starting Points

**Image manipulation software** provides a wealth of options for children to develop their ideas. Talk about how adding text and colour effects can enhance the feelings or message portrayed in the children's work. It is also good practice to encourage pupils to consider a title for their artwork.

## Approach

1. Load a saved scene from the last activity or **scan** in a charcoal drawing.

2. Explore the **colour filter** negative option; this reverses the colour values in the digital image.

3. Use different distortion filters to alter the appearance of the image and save the results.

4. Consider a title for the image. Use the text tool to apply a title on top of the image.

5. Experiment with font size and colour.

6. Save and print out.

# Mixed Media Boards

## Resources
- Computer connected to the Internet
- Manipulated printouts from the previous activity
- Card 180cm by 60cms
- PVA glue
- Coloured tissue paper
- Paint
- Oil pastel
- Digital camera

## Starting Points

Computer printouts can be used in different contexts; here they form the starting point for a large mixed-media composition. Artists such as Robert Rauschenburg and Kurt Schwitters use different materials and techniques including print, collage and painting in their compositions. Find out about these artists on the Internet (website suggestion page 72). Look at the children's manipulated computer printouts. Talk about how the ideas and emotions shown can be extended into a large composition using different materials.

## Approach

1. Glue the computer printout on to the centre of the card.

2. Using a mixture of thin PVA glue and tissue paper, apply areas of coloured tissue around the computer printout.

3. Layer different colours and overlap them around the edge of the printout.

4. Paint the remaining sections of the board, thinking carefully about choice of colour and its relationship to the central image and mood of the overall work.

5. Glue computer-generated text on to the board as a title.

6. Record the final mixed-media composition using a **digital camera**.

# Creating the Mobile

## Resources
- Computer connected to Internet
- A4 white paper
- Pens and pencils
- Thick card (25cm by 25cm)
- Ruler
- Scissors
- Collage material (local newspapers and magazines)
- Glue
- Paints or felt-tip pens

IMOOS, 1960–5 (gouache on card, wire, mirror and light set within painted wood box) by Bryan Wynter (1915–1975) 116.8 x 109.2cm, Whitworth Art Gallery, Manchester, UK © Estate of Bryan Wynter 2003. All Rights Reserved, DACS

## Starting Points

The modern world is full of moving elements such as people, transport and animals. Artists and sculptors throughout the twentieth century have been fascinated by the challenge of investigating and recording movement. Use the Internet to find out about artists such as Bryan Wynter and Alexander Calder, who created moving sculptures or mobiles (website suggestion on page 72). Bryan Wynter called his mobiles IMOOS (Images Moving Out Of Space) and displayed them in front of reflective surfaces.

## Approach

1. Create an IMOOS mobile. On white A4 paper, draw two squares. Divide each square into four equal strips using simple wavy, zigzag or straight lines.

2. On a piece of thick square card, carefully copy the design idea from the white paper.

3. Use the scissors to cut along the lines to create four different strips of card.

4. Join the four strips of card together (like a jigsaw puzzle) on a table and write 'collage' on each section in pencil.

5. Using local newspapers and magazines, cut out words and pictures that describe the area in which you live. Glue these carefully to the four sides marked 'collage'.

6. On the reverse side of the card, use felt-tip pens or paints to create contrasting colours and patterns.

# Constructing the Mobile

### Resources
- Metal clothes hangers
- Wire cutters
- Sharp craft knife
- Strips of card from the previous activity
- Compass
- Scissors
- Transparent nylon thread
- Tape
- Rulers

### Starting Points

Discuss the best way to construct a mobile. What materials have other artists used? Point out that it can be surprisingly difficult to make a well-balanced and aesthetically successful 'moving sculpture'.

*Untitled Mobile* by Alexander Calder (1898–1976), 1958, Christie's Images, London, UK/ Bridgeman Art Library © ARS, NY and DACS, London

### Approach

1. Prepare 30cm lengths of wire from old metal clothes hangers using wire cutters.

2. Arrange the four strips of cards on the table and decide which way up they will hang.

3. Place the card on a cutting mat and use the sharp point of the compass to make a hole close to the top of each strip of card.

4. Cut four 30cm pieces of nylon and thread each piece through the hole in the card and tie securely. Tie the other end of the thread to the length of wire.

5. Move the strips of card along the wire to achieve the correct balance and tape into place.

# Recording the Mobile

## Resources

- Children's constructed mobiles from the previous activity
- Coloured paper
- Pastels
- Digital camera
- A mirror or shiny paper
- Masking tape
- Image manipulation software

## Starting Points

Look again at the mobiles by Bryan Wynter and Alexander Calder (see page 44). Hang up the children's mobiles and talk about the best way to record movement. Experiment with drawing the moving mobiles using pastels. Discuss how it is easier to record the movement of the mobiles using a **digital camera**.

## Approach

1. Place a mirror or tape shiny reflective paper on a wall in the classroom and position the hanging mobile strips of card in front.

2. Turn each strip of card around at least ten times.

3. Record 12 still images of the moving mobile. Keep the camera perfectly still and press the button as quickly as possible over a short period of time.

4. If the digital camera can record a short film sequence, choose this option and record a five-second film sequence of the mobile.

5. Load the digital recordings on to the computer, select a favourite view and print out the result.

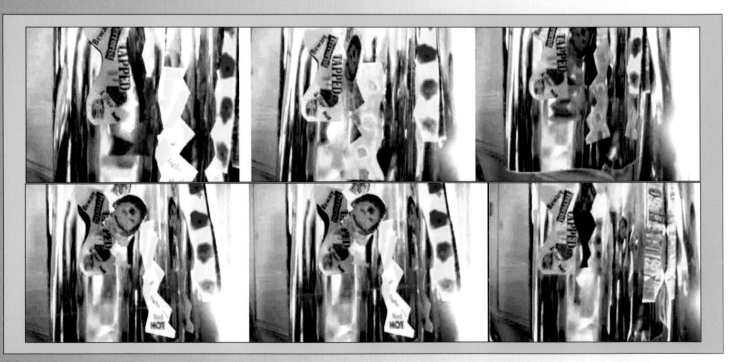

# Presenting the Recordings

## Resources

- Digital camera with saved mobile images from the previous activity
- Presentation software
- Paper
- Pencils

## Starting Points

Talk about how it is possible to display coursework in a range of different ways using computers. Presentation programs such as **PowerPoint** enable whole projects of combined and recorded text, images and digital video to be shown through a computer system. Demonstrate how to use presentation software. Discuss the importance of recording key stages of project work using a **digital camera**.

## Approach

1. Load and save the digital photographs from the project and previous activity onto thecomputer. Give each image an appropriate file name, such as 'movement 1'.

2. First, plan the presentation on a piece of paper. Divide the paper into a grid and write the sequence in each box. For example: Page 1 – title of project, Page 2 – mobile digital image.

3. Load a presentation program (for example, PowerPoint). This program will allow you to create a number of pages for your data.

4. Using the presentation program, insert the data onto the first page and then save the work.

5. Create a second page and repeat.

6. When all the data has been entered, present the screen-based display to the class.

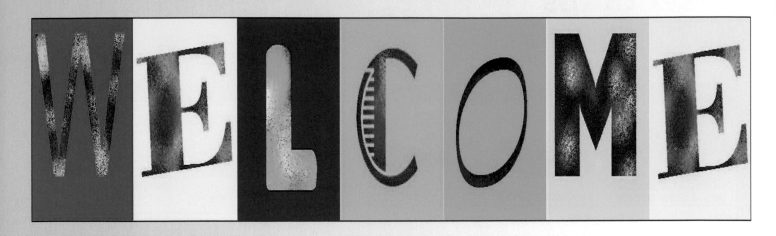

## Welcome Banners

### Resources
- Computer connected to the Internet
- Colour printer
- Newspapers
- Paper
- Glue
- Paint software
- Scissors

### Starting Points

Many graphic designers and artists use text to enhance their ideas. Talk about how we see text used daily in posters, magazines and on the Internet. Make a collection of magazine and newspaper font styles used for letters and numbers. Explain that different computer fonts are given names such as 'Arial' or 'Times'. Print out and examine various font styles. Look at different fonts found on the Internet (website suggestion page 72).

### Approach

1. Create a collage showing the word 'Welcome' in different languages. Cut out different large letters from newspapers and place them on a piece of paper.

2. Arrange the letters and glue them down.

3. Create a digital banner with each child allocated a different letter. Using paint software, open a new page and select portrait size.

4. Choose the font tool and type in a single letter. Set a large font size and choose a colour. Experiment with italic or bold, and upper case or lower case.

5. Use the colour fill tool to choose a background colour.

6. Save the letter and print it out.

7. Repeat with the other letters in the banner.

8. Join the printouts together to create the welcome banner.

9. Compare the banner created digitally with the original collage. What are the benefits of using the computer?

# Word Games

### Resources
- Examples of different fonts from magazines
- Paper
- Felt-tip pens
- Paint software

## Starting Points

Font manipulation is a technique used by graphic designers to attract attention. It often involves stretching, squashing and changing the form of words. Show examples of words found in magazines that explain their meaning through their appearance. Brainstorm appropriate words with the children and make a list. This is a good opportunity to talk about onomatopoeia – words that sound like their meaning.

## Approach

1. Choose a word to illustrate. Sketch ideas on to paper using felt-tips.

2. Use the text tool to set a large font size and type in the word.

3. Use distortion effects to change the shape of the word.

4. Experiment with the colour tool.

5. Print out the result.

6. Compare and contrast the sketches with the computer printout and discuss the differences.

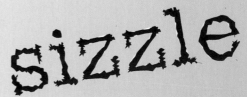

49

# Logos

## Resources
- Computer connected to the Internet
- A collection of logos from magazines and other resources
- Pencils
- Paints
- Plain paper
- Paint software
- Scissors
- Glue
- Scanner

## Starting Points

Talk about how logos are similar to badges. They are often used to celebrate and advertise the names of schools, companies and sporting teams. They usually comprise of a combination of words and pictures. Make a collection of logos from magazines and other products. Look for logos on the Internet (website suggestion page 72).

## Approach

1. Ask the children to design a personal logo with their name, favourite animal, sport, hobby or interest.

2. On A4 paper, paint a large symbol appropriate to (in this case) the school club.

3. Using a computer and paint software, type the required text using a large point size.

4. Experiment with colour and manipulation effects on the text.

5. Print out the results, and cut out and glue the letters along the edge of the shape, or glue the complete word to the painting.

6. Alternatively, **scan** the painting and save it on the computer. Experiment with manipulation effects, then type the text onto the image and print out.

# Illuminated Numbers

## Resources

- Magazines and newspapers
- Number frieze
- Computer connected to the Internet
- Paint software
- Glue
- Card

## Starting Points

Make a collection of the different styles of numbers found in magazines and newspapers. Look at the number frieze in your classroom and discuss the types of font used. In the Middle Ages, manuscripts were handwritten with beautiful illuminated letters. Look at some medieval numbers (website suggestion on page 72) and talk about the shapes and colours used.

## Approach

1. Open the paint software and create a portrait size page.

2. Use the font tool to choose a font style and colour, then type a number using a large point size. Save this.

3. Work in zoom mode and use different tools including pencil, paintbrush and spray can to decorate the letter using different marks and textures.

4. After decorating the number, experiment with the fill tool to choose an appropriate background colour.

5. Print out the number and glue onto card.

6. Arrange the numbers in order along the wall of the classroom to make a frieze.

# Building with Printouts

# A Walk Through the Town

## Starting Points

Plan a walk around local landmarks, places of interest and unusual features of the local area. Discuss the use of a digital camera to record the walk. Explain to the children that some software has a **layer feature** that allows images to be placed on top of each other and that each image can be modified without affecting the layer above or below. Demonstrate how to **cut and paste** between images, with particular emphasis on using the layer palette to fade images into each other.

## Approach

1. Walk through the local environment, taking photographs of various landmarks and interesting features using a **digital camera**.

2. Load the digital images onto the computer.

3. Choose one image to be the background for the collage. Use the software tools to adjust the **brightness and contrast** of this image and save it using a new name.

4. Open a second image and select a section from it. Cut and paste this section onto the background image. Repeat with a third image and place it on to the background image. The image will now have a background and two layers.

5. Save the image.

6. From the layer menu, choose each layer in turn and experiment by changing its colour and intensity using the colour and contrast tools.

7. Print and save the final image.

# Map Box Frame

## Resources

- Cardboard box lids A4 size
- Photocopied maps of the local area
- Scissors
- Paints
- Digital camera
- Image manipulation software
- Digital collages from previous activity
- Coloured paper
- Glue

## Starting Points

Talk about the fact that most artists give their work a frame. Can the children suggest how best to frame their pictures of the local area? Can they think of a way to use a 3-D effect?

## Approach

1. Make an original frame for the printouts. Line the cardboard lid with photocopied maps of the local area. Cover the entire lid, including the edges.

2. Apply a coloured wash using paint diluted with water over the entire lid and leave it to dry.

3. Photograph each child's face using the **digital camera** and load these on to the computer. Open the saved digital collage from the previous activity. Cut and paste the face onto the collage.

4. Save and print out the final result.

5. Glue a sheet of coloured paper into the bottom of the box. Next, glue the computer printout on to the paper.

6. Construct different shapes with the boxes to make an interesting display.

# A Journey Through the Woods

## Resources
- Digital images of wooded areas
- Sweets
- Digital camera
- Image manipulation software

## Approach

1. Load the images of the local environment on to the computer.

2. Arrange the sweets and take photographs of them using the **digital camera**. Load these images onto the computer.

3. Open one woodland image and one sweet image.

4. Use the cut and paste tools to place the sweets into the woodland image.

5. Save the image using a new name.

6. Use the capacity option in the layer palette to merge the sweets into the background.

7. Save and print the final image.

## Starting Points

Start by showing the children a variety of digital images of wooded areas. Tell the story of *Hansel and Gretel* who, on a walk through the woods, came upon a house covered with sweet things (website suggestion page 72). Explain to the children that they are going to create digital images using photographs of woodland areas and hide sweets within these images using the **layer feature**. Demonstrate how to **cut and paste** and **flatten** the images to merge layers.

# Hansel and Gretel House

## Starting Points

Retell the story of *Hansel and Gretel*. Ask the children to describe the cottage and to imagine how it looked when covered with different sweet patterns, like wallpaper. Talk about using **cut and paste** tools to create a sweet wallpaper pattern. Experiment with **colour filters** and effects.

## Approach

1. Open a sweet image.

2. Cut out one or a group of sweets and repeat using the repeat pattern function or paste several times to create a wallpaper effect.

3. Use **colour filters** to modify the colour of the sweets.

4. Save and print the images ready to glue onto the house.

5. Use cardboard boxes to create the main structure of the cottage.

6. Add details using cardboard strips for windows and doors.

7. Cover every part of the cottage with the sweet printouts.

# Creating a Storyboard

*Red and Black Streams*, 1973 (oil on canvas) by Bryan Wynter (1915–1975) 182.8 x 274.8cm,
Private Collection © Estate of Bryan Wynter 2003. All Rights Reserved DACS

## Starting Points

Use the Internet to find out about Bryan Wynter (website suggestion page 72). This artist made paintings based on movement using streams, rivers and the sea as his subject. Explain that Bryan Wynter lived by the sea and rowed his glass-bottomed canoe to gain a first-hand experience of water movement on the coastline. Discuss the challenge facing artists trying to create the effect of different types of movement on canvas.

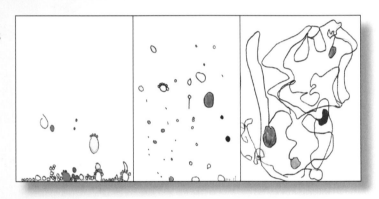

## Approach

1. Introduce **storyboard** drawing – explain that it involves drawing quickly in frames to show a sequence of movement that happens over a short period of time. Create a simple storyboard grid by dividing an A4 piece of paper into three sections.

2. Fill a shallow tray with water and add a few drops of coloured marbling ink. Stir the water and watch it move as the ink changes shape.

3. Every minute, produce one line drawing in pen, of the moving water on each section of the grid.

4. Investigate water movement further by visiting a swimming pool, a stream or the sea. Children could make a series of quick sketchbook drawings using a storyboard frame or use pastels to create movement pictures.

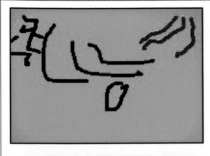
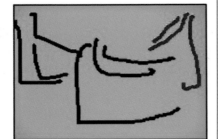
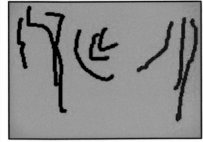
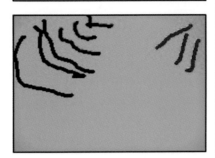
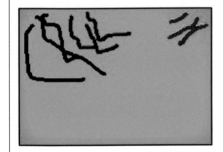
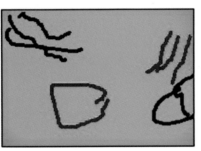

# Animated Water

## Resources
- Cartoon flipbooks
- Water storyboard from the previous activity
- Animation software
- Data projector

## Starting Points

Discuss **storyboards** and how animators such as Walt Disney have used storyboards to create animated cartoons. Explain that before computers were used, every frame in a film was hand-drawn. This involved drawing 25 frames for every second of film. Demonstrate this with a cartoon flipbook. Show how computers can store and play back information through the use of appropriate **animation software**.

## Approach

1. Create six frames and then use the water storyboard from the last activity to draw water moving within each frame using the **mouse**. Try to make the individual drawings different in each frame.

2. Save the film onto the hard disk and then play it back and view the action.

3. The sequence can be edited in a number of different ways. For example, if you want to slow down the film, you can duplicate several of the frames in a sequence.

4. Print out the frames.

5. Join individual frames together to create a group or class film that can be played back on the screen or to an audience by attaching the computer to a data projector.

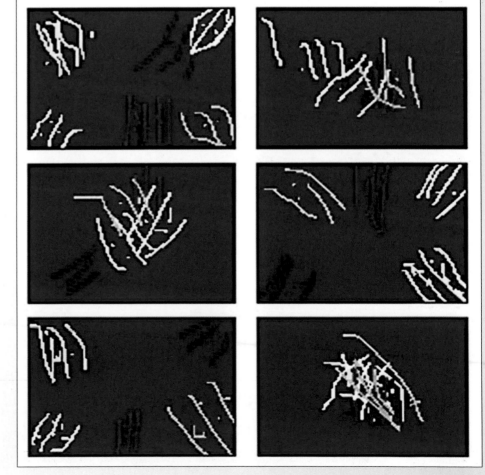

# Acrylic Water Panels

## Resources
- Computer connected to the Internet
- Water storyboards from the activity on page 56
- Cardboard squares (30cm by 30cm)
- Pencils
- Acrylic paints
- Sponges
- Sticks

## Approach

1. Use the **storyboard** printouts as a starting point for a water drawing in pencil on a square of card.

2. Discuss background colours that give a watery effect. Apply a coloured background using sponges dipped in acrylic paint thinned with water. Allow to dry.

3. Use undiluted acrylic paint and thin sticks to draw in the river details on the surface. Allow to dry.

4. Experiment with moving the panels to different configurations, for example a long single line, diamond or circle.

5. Choose spaces in the school to display the panels; for example, around a door. Change the installation frequently using the walls, floors and ceilings in different locations each week.

## Starting Points

Use the Internet to find out about interactive artists such as Andy Goldsworthy and Carl André (website suggestions page 72). These artists present their work as site specific installations. Explain the term 'interactive' as a flexible display that can be arranged by others. Discuss the ways in which symmetrical shapes can be arranged in different ways as an installation.

# Panel Presentation

## Resources
- Acrylic panels from the previous activity
- Digital camera
- Presentation software

## Starting Points

Demonstrate how information can be presented on a computer system using presentation software. What advantages does a computer system have in presenting artwork? Talk about the ways in which presentation software enables children to display their work, including text and video. Discuss how to use the water panels to make a computer-generated presentation.

## Approach

1. Experiment with different configurations of panels on the floor and record each one with a **digital camera**.

2. Save these images on to the hard disk.

3. Load a presentation program like **PowerPoint** and insert a configuration onto the first page, then save.

4. Scale the picture to the required size and position.

5. Use **crop** to cut around the squares exactly. This will eliminate the background.

6. Create a second page and repeat with another configuration. Repeat until all configurations have been recorded.

7. Finally, click on each square and press the right-hand **mouse** button, and then **custom animation**. This creates an animated effect for each square, such as a spiral or fly.

8. Save your presentation and play it back to an audience.

9. As a class, compare the differences between a real and a screen-based presentation.

# Designing the Character

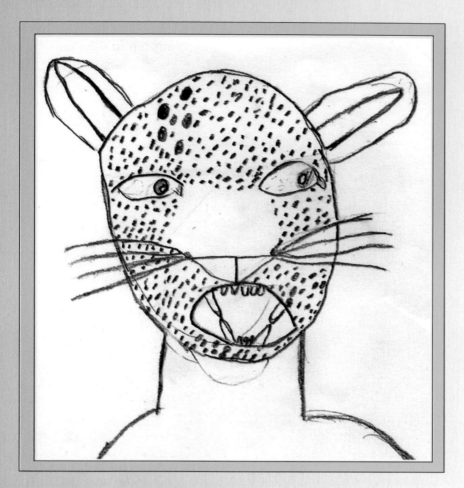

### Resources
- Computer connected to the Internet
- White paper
- Charcoal
- Pencils

## Starting Points

Computer games are part of contemporary culture and are used by many children. Ask the children to name different types of game characters and to describe them. Explain to the class that they are going to design a character for a new computer game. Ask them to imagine the type of character – cartoon, human, animal, good or evil. Use the Internet to look at existing game characters as a prompt (website suggestion page 72).

## Approach

1. Ask the children to make drawings of each other in different poses from different viewpoints, and to explore how the character might walk, stand and sit.

2. Work in pairs to develop drawings showing different expressions – angry, sad, happy.

3. Simplify the drawings to develop a new character and use imagination to distort the facial features.

4. As an alternative, combine some existing game characters to create a new character in charcoal.

5. Consider the costume for the character. Discuss the costumes worn on existing game characters and use these to support the development of ideas.

# Digital Character

## Resources
- Computer connected to the Internet
- Children's game character drawings from the previous activity
- Scanner
- Digital camera
- Image manipulation software

## Starting Points

Look again at some existing game characters (website suggestion page 72). What special effects are achieved through using digital software? Discuss with the children how they could enhance their character drawings. Demonstrate how to **scan** a character image into the computer. Talk about using the **software tools** to enhance their designs by applying different colours and textures.

## Approach

1. Take photographs of different textures and patterns found around the school using the **digital camera**, and load these onto the computer.

2. Scan and load a game character design onto the computer.

3. Open a texture image. Use the **cut and paste** tools to paste different textures into parts of the design.

4. Continue the process by adding colour and detail using the drawing and painting tools. Save and print out the final design.

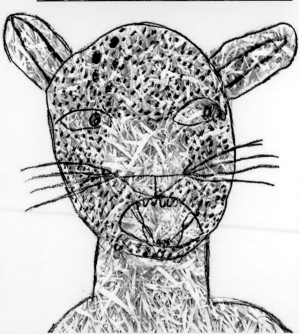

# Creating Different Worlds

## Resources
- White paper
- Drawing materials
- Paints or pastels
- Scanner
- Image manipulation software

## Starting Points

Talk about the different kinds of environment or worlds found in computer games. Look at some existing game environments. Talk about composition, atmosphere, historical places and futuristic spaces. Look at the landscapes of different artists past and present, and discuss how game designers take inspiration from many different sources.

## Approach

1. Make a series of sketches of different urban and rural environments, and choose one design that suits the character.

2. Complete the design using paints or pastels. Remind the children to pay particular attention to colour and pattern when creating the landscape.

3. **Scan** the design into the computer and add colours and textures using the **mouse**. Experiment with the effects of different paint tools.

4. Consider the mood or atmosphere in the environment and use colour to enhance these feelings and to give drama to the design.

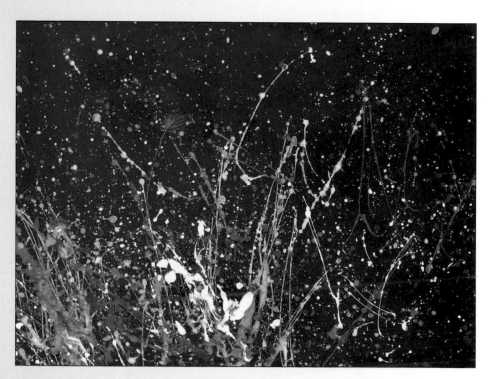

# Adding the Character to the Background

## Resources
- Digital images from page 61
- Digital camera
- Colour printer

## Starting Points

Talk about adding the game character to the background of an image. Discuss scale – how big should the character look? Discuss adding detail to the character, such as shadows and effects that might make the image look more dramatic.

## Approach

1. Open a background and character image.

2. Using **cut and paste**, cut out the character and paste it on to the environment.

3. Save the image using a new name.

4. Experiment with the scale.

5. Use a range of different tools and effects to add detail to the image.

6. Save and print the image.

7. For an extension activity, ask the children to photograph each other in a game pose using the **digital camera**. Load these images onto the computer and then cut and paste an image onto the digital background following steps 2–6 above.

# Multimedia Presentation

# Planning the Presentation

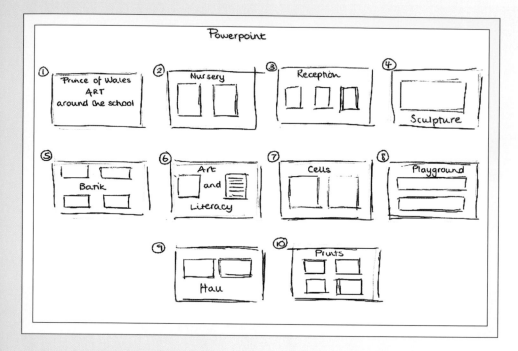

## Resources

- Presentation software with an example slide show
- Pencils and pens
- Paper
- Ruler

## Starting Points

Show the children an example **PowerPoint** slide show. Talk about creating a presentation to show the different aspects of the school. Introduce a **storyboard** as a tool for planning a presentation. Talk about the ways in which storyboards are used in the film industry to plan out a sequence of events. Explain that the storyboard will be the template for taking a series of photographs with the **digital camera** for the presentation.

## Approach

1. In groups, walk around the school selecting different areas to include in the presentation. Make sketches and notes on a storyboard to create a sequence plan for the presentation.

2. Discuss possible photographs to take in each area. Consider different viewpoints – some long shots and some close-ups will make the presentation more varied and interesting.

3. Back in the classroom, look again at the storyboard notes. Compare ideas as a class and make any revisions of sequence.

4. Decide on the text captions for each frame and write these onto the storyboard.

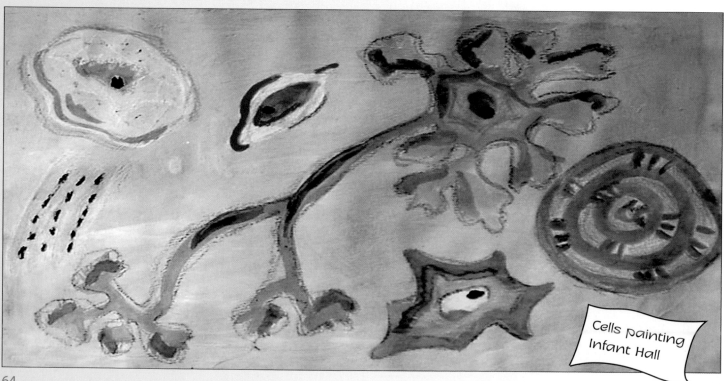

Cells Painting
Infant Hall

# Taking the Photographs

## Resources
- Completed storyboards from the previous activity
- Digital camera
- Image manipulation software

## Approach

1. Using the storyboards as a guide, walk around the school in groups and take photographs using the digital camera.

2. Experiment with photographing the same scene from different viewpoints.

3. Load and save the images onto the computer.

4. View the images and make a selection of the 20 that are most interesting.

## Starting Points

Display and discuss the **storyboards**. Question the children about the sequence of images and text captions. Demonstrate how to use the **digital camera**. Look at a sequence of images from different viewpoints and discuss which looks the best. Talk about the importance of using different camera angles to make the presentation more interesting. Demonstrate how to load the digital camera images onto the computer.

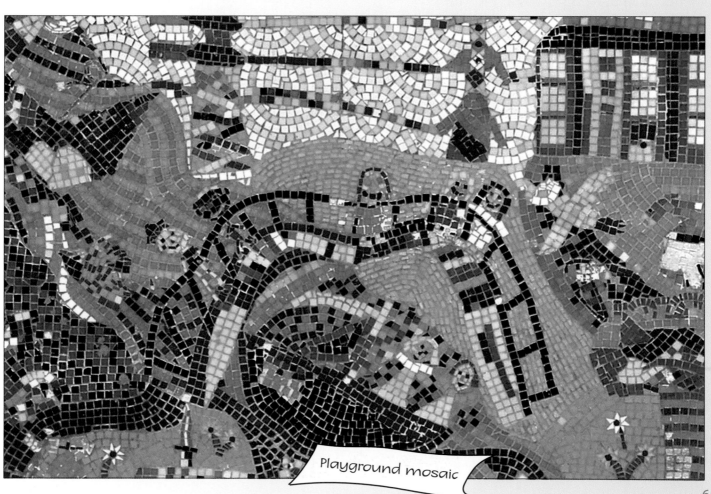

Playground mosaic

65

# Editing the Pictures

## Resources
- Loaded digital photographs of the school environment from the previous activity
- Image manipulation software
- Presentation software

## Starting Points

Talk to the children about their photographs and discuss the composition of the images. Think about **cropping** some of the images to remove unnecessary information. Demonstrate how to crop an image and how to make adjustments to the **brightness and contrast**. Demonstrate how to change the size of an image and how to create a **PowerPoint** screen.

## Approach

1. View each image in turn and make decisions about the composition. Crop the images as necessary.

2. Resave all of the cropped/saved images using a new name and save them in a new folder on the hard drive.

3. Adjust the brightness and contrast of each image if necessary. Experiment with **colour filters** and effects.

4. Insert the images into a PowerPoint screen. Add the text.

# Creating the Presentation

Indian Textile

Masks

Cells

## Resources

- Presentation software
- Completed storyboards from the activity on page 64
- An example slide show
- Loaded digital photographs from around the school from the activity on page 66

## Approach

1. Open a new 20-page presentation. Save the presentation.

2. Working from the **storyboard**, insert the edited images from the last activity onto each page.

3. Animate the text and images.

4. Experiment with changing the background colour and the text colour.

5. Play the presentation and make final adjustments to the animation.

## Starting Points

Explain to the children that presentation software can be used to create a slide show including text, sound, images and video. Look again at an example slide show and discuss the effects included. Start a new **PowerPoint** presentation and demonstrate how to input text and insert digital pictures. Animate the images and demonstrate how to alter the colour and size of the text. Explore how to delete and add new frames to the presentation.

## Additional activities

Add a soundtrack to the presentation. This could be music or a voice-over that describes the content of each page. Voices can be recorded by connecting a microphone to the computer and recording through the recording tools in the presentation software. Some software also contains sample music clips that can be played alongside a sequence of frames.

# Designing the Gallery

### Resources
- Computer connected to the Internet
- Pencils and paper

## Starting Points

A website is a collection of electronic pages that can include text, image, sound, animation and video. Websites are accessed through a **web browser**. Look at some gallery websites on the Internet (website suggestion page 72). Talk about creating an electronic art gallery using the children's art. Discuss how to move from page to page in a website. Note that the first page is called the **splash page**, which generally gives the name of the site and an image and the second is the **homepage** from where links can be made to other pages. The finished web pages can be viewed using the school's **Intranet** or Internet site.

*Prince of Wales Primary School*

Click here to enter

*Web Art Gallery*

## Approach

1. Look at splash pages and homepages of existing websites and discuss their function.

2. Discuss a suitable image for the art gallery splash page. Record these ideas on paper.

3. Ask the children to design a simple homepage for the gallery on paper. What text and images are needed? The homepage could contain links to four pages: gallery one (painting), gallery two (sculpture), gallery three (digital art) and a links page.

4. Design each gallery page on paper. Share all the designs with the class and decide on a final splash page, homepage and gallery page design.

*Prince of Wales Primary School*

gallery 1 | gallery2 | gallery3 | links
Welcome to our Art Gallery    click on the words to view the pictures

gallery 1 - painting
gallery 2 - sculpture
gallery 3 - digital art
Powerpoint Presentation

gallery 1 | gallery2 | gallery3 | links
*Web Art Gallery*

# Creating the Web Art Gallery

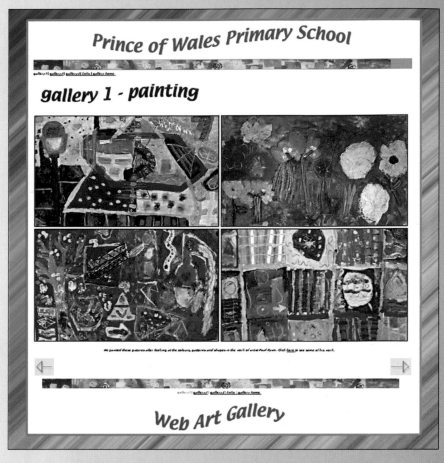

Web Art Gallery

## Resources
- Web design software
- Image manipulation software
- Children's designs from the previous activity
- Scanner
- Digital camera

## Starting Points

Talk about web design software where text and images are entered onto a page. Some software will provide you with ready-made templates or you can create your own. Using the children's designs, photograph the artwork with a **digital camera**. Alternatively, work can be **scanned** into the computer. Crop and resize the images using **image manipulation software** ready for inclusion on the web page. Edit the images to make them all the same size. **All the website information should be stored in the same folder.** Demonstrate how to create a new page and how to insert images and text.

## Approach

1. Create the **splash page** by inserting a single image onto the template and add the name of the school.

2. Create another new page – this will be the **homepage** of the site – and add images and text.

3. Create a separate page for each gallery using the same template but saving each new page using a different name, for example gallery 1, gallery 2, and so on.

4. From the homepage, make the links (**hyperlinks**) to the gallery pages. From the splash page, make a link to the homepage.

5. Using the same method of linking pages, insert a 'back' or 'previous page' button so that you can move freely between the pages.

# Art Slide Show

## Resources
- Web design software
- Presentation software

## Starting Points

Start by creating a multimedia presentation (see pages 64–67). Explain that it is possible to add existing documents or materials to the art website. These can be word-processing documents or multimedia presentations.

## Approach

1. Open an existing multimedia presentation.

2. From the file menu, choose the 'save as web page' option. Follow the on-screen instructions. The choices you make will determine the look of the presentation on the web page.

3. Save the presentation in the same folder as the art website pages.

4. From the homepage, make a link to the presentation.

5. Preview the presentation on the website.

# Linking Up

## Resources
- Computer connected to the Internet
- Web design software

## Starting Points

Talk about adding links from your website to another site. List the types of websites that would be relevant, such as other schools, children's art clubs and art galleries. Look at some websites on the Internet and decide which would be suitable as a link. It is good practice to send an email to the website link to ask permission. Check that the content of the linking website is suitable. Demonstrate how to create a new page for the links and how to link to another site.

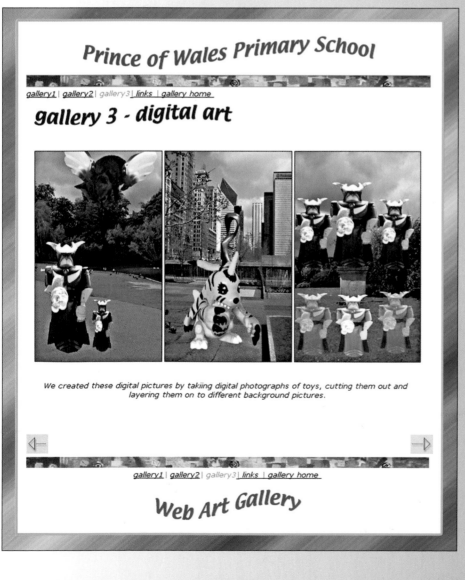

*We created these digital pictures by takiing digital photographs of toys, cutting them out and layering them on to different background pictures.*

## Approach

1. Using web design software, create another web page entitled 'Useful Links'. You may choose to modify one of the existing pages.

2. On this page, add the links (**hyperlinks**) to the other websites by simply typing in the relevant website addresses. These links will only work when the computer is connected to the Internet.

3. View the new page and check that the links work.

## Additional Activities

The completed web pages can be viewed on the school **intranet** using a **web browser**. In order to make the website accessible to others outside the school, it will need to be loaded on to a server and will need to have a unique address, for example www.myartgallery.co.uk. You will need to work collaboratively with the IT coordinator to add your pages to the school website.

## Website Suggestions

**Looking at Landscape**
www.ibiblio.org/wm/paint/auth/hockney/
www.geocities.com/CapeCanaveral/2933/fauves/

**Mythical Creatures**
www.mythicalrealm.com/
www.pantheon.org/mythica.html
www.eaudrey.com/myth/index.html
www.mythcreatures.50megs.com/index.htm

**Sculpture in Landscape**
www.henry-moore-fdn.co.uk
www.cgee.hamline.edu/see/goldsworthy/see_an_andy.htlm
www.richardlong.org/

**Cave Art**
www.culture.fr/culture/arcnat/lascaux/en/index4.htlm
www.clipart4schools.com

**Out of this World**
www.claytonbailey.com/robogroup.htm
www.drumcroon.org.uk
http://android.members.beeb.net/Information.htlm

**Acetate Birds**
www.ncl.ac.uk/hatton/collection/mixed-media/

**Pop Portraits**
www.artcyclopedia.com/artists/paolozzi_eduardo.html
www.tomphillips.co.uk/sculptur/
www.artcyclopedia.com/artists/warhol_andy.html
www.cln.org/themes/masks.html

**Natural Patterns**
www.artchive.com/artchive/ftptoc/okeefe_ext.html

**Folk Art**
www.comptonverney.co.uk/index.asp
www.artcyclopedia.com/artists/rauschenberg_robert.html
www.artcyclopedia.com/artists/schwitters_kurt.html

**Moving Mobiles**
www.24hourmuseum.org.uk/nwh/ART9819.html
www.sfmoma.org/espace/calder/calder_earlymobiles.html

**Transforming Text**
www.abstractfonts.com
school.diskovery.com/clipart
www.retrokat.com/medieval/leil.htm

**Building with Printouts**
www.surlalunefairytales.com/hanselgretel/
index.html#THIRTY5RE

**Water Feature**
www.artcyclopedia.com/artists/goldsworthy_andy.html
www.artcyclopedia.com/artists/andre_carl.html

**Game Character**
www.gameonweb.co.uk/education/intro.html

**Web Art Gallery**
www.artcyclopedia.com/

## Suggested software

**Animation Software**
The Complete Animator (PC only): www.iota.co.uk/products/tca/
Animationshop supplied with Paintshop-Pro (PC only): www.digitalworkshop.co.uk

**Image Manipulation Software (with layers)**
Adobe Photoshop Elements (Mac/PC): www.adobe.co.uk/products/photoshopel/main.html
Paintshop-Pro (PC only): www.digitalworkshop.co.uk

**Paint Software**
Dazzle Plus (PC only): www.granada-learning.com
Revelation Natural Art (PC only): www.logo.com/cat/view/revelation-natural-art.html

**Web Design and Presentation Software**
Microsoft Front Page (Mac/PC): www.microsoft.com
Microsoft PowerPoint (Mac/PC): http://search.office.microsoft.com